Be More Bee

HOW TO FIND YOUR BUZZ

ALISON DAVIES

Illustrations by Emily Mayor

Hardie Grant

QUADRILLE

'Books are the bees
which carry the
quickening pollen from
one to another mind.'

JAMES RUSSELL LOWELL

Introduction

I am something of a bee whisperer. It started
when I was five years old and on holiday with
my parents. Instead of playing with the other
children one afternoon, I was more enamoured
with a giant bumble bee I found sitting on the
window ledge. Bulbous and bountiful in its beauty,
this seaside bee appeared to have more attitude
than its urban cousin. With puffed-out fur and
golden stripes that wouldn't look out of place on
the catwalk, it was beatific in its radiance and that
made me want to reach out and stroke it, to steal
some of that dynamic energy myself. So I did –
gently, of course – and I can still remember the
softness to this day, and the feeling of connection
with such an amazing creature. I have been
stroking bees ever since (if they'll let me).

You see, for me the bee has everything. It's a
magical marvel, a creature of flair and talent,
a friend of the earth and an advocate of girl
power. It's a totem. A conundrum.

A symbol of fascination since the beginning of time, the bee always plays fair by offering a helpful antenna. Most importantly, though, it shares the love and the hard-won sugary spoils in the form of cure-all superfood honey.

I haven't even mentioned the dance moves yet, but let me tell you, they are the bee's knees and reveal far more than a buzzing sense of rhythm.

Yes, bees truly are an inspiration, as this book will attest. Whether you're a fan or a sceptic, these winged wonders will delight you with their wisdom and teach you how to fly higher than you thought possible. All you have to do is open your heart and mind and **be more bee**!

'Those bees, which chose thy sweet mouth for their hive, to gather honey from thy works, survive.'

THOMAS PECKE

Immortality

Bees are nature's alchemists. They spin straw to gold when they produce all-round superfood and nectar to the gods, honey. Though it sounds like the plot of a fairy tale, these magical creatures rely little on enchantment and more on sheer hard work and industry to make the miracle happen. Yet several scientific processes are at play during the creation of this wonder stuff.

Once the bees have gathered enough nectar in their aptly named 'honey stomachs', internal enzymes set to work, breaking down the sugars, making them less prone to crystallisation. On arrival back at the hive, a speedy game of 'pass the sugar parcel' begins, as the older worker bees regurgitate the substance for the younger house bees to consume. They also have enzymes which break down the sugar, and they pass the parcel between them until they've reduced the water content by around 20 per cent. At this point the final house bee will deposit the prize in a honeycomb cell, and the hive bee steps in to admire its magnificence and fan the substance with powerful wings, thus evaporating any remaining water and transforming it into honey. The cell is capped off with beeswax, leaving the golden stuff safely stored for consumption. Job done!

It's a teamwork marvel, and a model of organisation that has worked for centuries, serving bees and humans alike. For while bees need honey to survive the harsh winter months, humans enjoy its benefits too. The rich sugariness is treat enough when spread on toast, but there's more to this glistening delicacy than how it tastes. Honey contains all of the substances needed to sustain life, including enzymes, water, minerals and vitamins. The Ancient Egyptians loved it so much that pots were taken to the grave and have since been unearthed in tombs dating back 3,000 years. Even more surprising, it's still perfectly edible and sweet to the taste. Hard to bee-lieve, but the buzz is true: honey withstands all things. High in antioxidants and with anti-inflammatory properties, it can be used to lower blood pressure, boost the immune system and treat wounds, something the Egyptians did with gusto. No wonder they thought it the perfect gift for the dearly departed, who might need patching up, or at the very least a sugary snack, for the journey to the afterlife.

But let's not forget the bees. Without their selfless brilliance, one of our most loved condiments might cease to exist. Worker bees may only live a few weeks, but in that short time they work miracles, creating around one-twelfth of a teaspoon of honey, which when added to the hive's pot comes to around 90 kilograms a year. Bees mean business. They worry not about themselves, about their short life span, or the things they need to get done and the time they have to do it. They take their vision and make it a reality. Daring to dream, and going for it, big style. The ethos of the bee is simple: to bee-lieve is to achieve!

Be more bee

All good magicians, alchemists and bees know that a spell is a combination of intention, effort and belief. Without a balance of these three things there is no golden prize at the end. Keep this in mind to help you manifest your dreams.

● Make clear your intention: what do you want and why do you want it?
● Identify the physical steps you must take and take them.
● Believe you can and will succeed.

Even when you've done all you can do and the chips are down – believe, believe and bee-lieve some more.

Spin straw into gold

Never ones to shy away from hard work, bees know that the tastiest honey is worth the effort. They might have to forage further afield, carry more nectar and generally stretch themselves in order to produce it, but that just makes it taste even sweeter. And you too can create magic, by channelling the worker bee focus and spirit.

STEP ONE

Start by imagining your life in a few years' time. Where do you want to be, and what do you want to be doing? Write a short paragraph describing your life as you'd like it to be.

STEP TWO

Research the best way to get the life you want. Do you need special skills or training? Perhaps you need to work out a way to save more money, or earn more money? What steps can you take to do this? Write down at least five actions that will take you closer to your goal.

STEP THREE

Spread the word. Tell your nearest and dearest about your plans. Let them help and encourage you, while also keeping you on track and focused.

STEP FOUR

Find a mentor, someone you admire who has the type of skills and knowledge that you need to succeed. Watch and learn from them. Get experience when you can and don't be afraid to start at the bottom.

STEP FIVE

If you feel your determination starting to slip, keep the end goal in mind. Read through the paragraph you wrote in Step One describing your life in a few years' time and visualise it in your mind. Imagine how you'll feel when you reach this point. Then give yourself a pat on the back for the work you've done so far.

Harness your honey

If you had a magical power, what would it be? Bees, as superior beings, have many, from their ability to sense nectar, to their internal workings which help turn sugar into gold. What's your magical potential? Think qualities rather than talents or skills – what makes you unique? If you're struggling to think of an answer, ask a trusted friend what they like about you. Anything from the way you laugh to your thoughtful manner can go on the list. All of these things work together to create the special magic that is you. Acknowledge these beautiful quirks and traits. Give thanks for them every day and you'll build self-esteem, which in turn will help your individual brand of magic to shine through.

Be more bee

Find your buzz by repeating a positive affirmation in a chant. Start with something simple like 'I love me,' and repeat it continuously, getting louder and faster each time. Then bring it back down to a quieter, gentler rhythm and add in something else like 'I love life,' so in this case you'd say 'I love me, I love life, I love me, I love life,' on a loop, getting louder and faster as you go. A minute of chanting should raise energy levels and also make you feel inspired and ready to take on the world.

'The reason that fish form schools, birds form flocks, and bees form swarms is that they are smarter together than they would be apart. They don't take a vote; they don't take a poll: they form a system. They are all interactive and make a decision together in real time.'

LOUIS B. ROSENBERG

Be the dream team

'Together' is the bee's mantra. It's the word that means the most, for all things are completed with ease if everyone pulls together and plays their part. Working as a team may have its challenges, but it can also bring new opportunities and maximise success and happiness. Treat the world as your team and every person you meet as a valued member. Know that everyone has something to offer. We are all connected, like the cells in a hive. We might live separately, but we are intrinsically linked, whether family, friends or colleagues. Everything we do has an effect. With this in mind, get behind your team with these bee-inspired tips.

● Identify the role you play with others. Are you the ideas person, the mischief-maker, the motivator, or the one who empathises and offers support? Play to your talents and strengths in both your work and leisure time.

● Identify the roles others play in the team. When you're aware of where others fit, you know who to turn to, and when.

● Be open and maintain the flow of communication with your team members. Ask them how they feel and talk about what's going on in their lives. At the same time, be open about how you feel and what's important to you.

● Everyone should feel valued in a team, so make sure you give praise when it's deserved, and encouragement when it's needed.

● Remember your animal dream team too, from beloved pets to the wildlife on your doorstep. Treat animals like members of the gang. They're just as much a part of your tribe and will help you be more effective and fulfilled in what you do, so spend time with pets and share the love, feed the birds, grow bee-friendly plants and flowers, and value the creatures in your life.

Be more bee

Bees have teamwork sussed. Their animal instincts are fine-tuned, meaning they know what to do and when to do it to get the best results. We aren't quite as on the ball, but we can improve the way we intuitively gel with others by playing together. Get involved in group activities, from playing sports to working towards challenges like running a marathon. Doing something fun that involves practice, skill and a universal goal helps you bond and form connections, while improving body language and communication skills.

WORDS

—

Get busy with it

Be the miracle

Bee-lieve to achieve

Now is when it happens

Teamwork is dream work

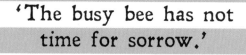

'The busy bee has not
time for sorrow.'

WILLIAM BLAKE

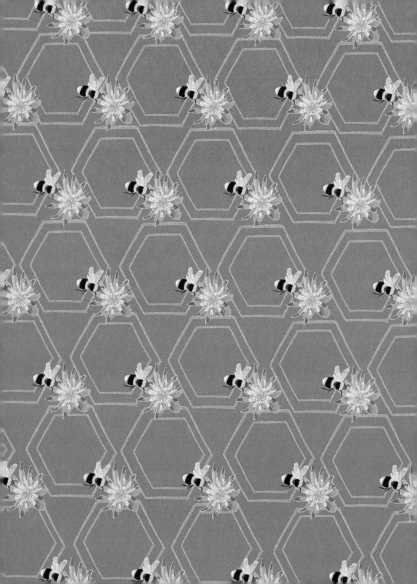

Staying Alive

The honey bee, a supreme being, has also been a thing of mystery for many years. Perplexing science and defying the odds, her body-to-wing ratio means she shouldn't be able to take off, let alone travel 3 metres per second in search of sustenance. But this lady neither gives up nor shirks her responsibilities. The fact she shouldn't be able to do something matters not. She does it anyway, to prove a point and fly in the face of non-believers.

For centuries we humans, in our confused state, have tried to draw comparisons between bees and other airborne creatures. But make no mistake, bees are not birds, or flies, or aeroplanes. Bees are bees, and that is enough. They operate on an entirely different level. Their wings may be tiny compared to their bootylicious derrières, but that's what ensures that they're up to the job of carrying hefty loads of pollen.

Think of the bee as the powerlifting champion of the bug kingdom. Her wings move independently, and being more flexible than her avian cousins, they rotate, wiggle and flap at a rate of around 230 times a second, creating a vortex of air which propels her onwards and upwards with force. This super rapid wingbeat allows her to hover, load and transfer her bounty with ease. Even so, she must travel over 55,000 miles and tap around 2 million flowers to make 450 grams of honey. Flying 24 kilometres in an hour and visiting between 50 and 100 flower heads each time, it's an Olympic task,

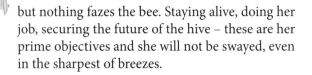

but nothing fazes the bee. Staying alive, doing her job, securing the future of the hive – these are her prime objectives and she will not be swayed, even in the sharpest of breezes.

No wonder the Native Americans recognise the bee as a powerful totem and ally. What she lacks in size, she makes up for in energy, going above and beyond what is required to achieve the seemingly impossible. Science, magic, or a combination of both? It matters not to the humble bumble. She just gets on with it. A flying force of nature, turbo-charged and ready to take on the world; tenacious bee is the word.

Be more bee

Fans of hovering, bees understand that sometimes you need to stop, chill and assess the situation from above. If you feel you're not making progress in some area of your life, try hovering instead of stressing. Take a step back and imagine you're looking down on the situation from a great height. You can see what's going on with you and anyone else involved. You can see the bigger picture and how events in your world relate to everything else. You notice that the universe is vast, and that you and the situation you are facing is just one tiny part of the web. Breathe, relax and give yourself a moment to take this in. Adding some perspective is often enough to spark a solution, or a way to move forwards.

Find your wings

While we aren't physically blessed with wings, we can still fly high and get to where we want to be with bee-like ingenuity!

⬡ The bee has adapted the use of its wings so that it can fly great distances. What, if anything, do you need to adapt to reach your destination? Look into alternative routes. Talk to those who've gone before and work out a plan B and C so that you have a number of options available.

⬡ Don't limit yourself. Instead of talking yourself down, be sure to focus on your skills and talents. Remove the phrase 'I can't' from your vocabulary and replace it with 'I can, and I will!'

● Be tenacious. Don't give up at the first, second or third hurdle. If things don't go your way, treat it as a lesson and consider what you've learnt and what you'll do differently next time.

● Act as if you're already where you want to be. Be confident in your own abilities, and if you're facing a brick wall, trust in yourself and rise above it.

Pump up the power

A honey bee in flight creates a flow of static electricity, which attracts pollen and helps it stick to her hairy body. By pumping up the power, she's able to carry a maximum load, and pollinate other plants as she goes. Follow suit and create an instant buzz by powering up your energy.

STEP ONE
Give yourself the brush down. Using brisk sweeping strokes, brush your hands down from the top of your head over each shoulder and down your arms with the palms of your hands. Imagine you're brushing away negative energy and encouraging the flow of blood around your body.

STEP TWO
Continue brushing down your stomach and legs, then give your entire body a good shake.

STEP THREE
Visualise yourself standing in a shower of bright white light. Feel it hitting the top of your head and washing over you, giving you an instant energy boost.

Be more bee

Bees use every bit of their body when foraging, so it's important they're in tip-top shape and take care that everything is working as it should. Do the same and check in regularly with your body throughout the day. Notice how you feel and if there's any tension anywhere. Flex and stretch each muscle group in turn and adjust your posture so that you're standing or sitting with your spine lengthened and your shoulders relaxed.

The men of experiment
are like the ant; they
only collect and use.
But the bee... gathers
its materials from the
flowers of the garden
and of the field, but
transforms and digests it
by a power of its own.'

LEONARDO DA VINCI

Harness the nectar

Imagine you had two stomachs, one for eating and one for storing and transporting food. Such is the life of the honey bee, who has an eating belly, and a backpack belly, which when full weighs almost the same as she does! It might sound like hard work, but she's simply making the most of her assets and gathering as much nectar as she can, while she can.

Identify the nectar in your life. Ask yourself:

- What gives me a buzz?
- What do I really enjoy doing?
- What makes me feel proud?

Then think of ways in which you can introduce more of this into your everyday routine. Perhaps you're an adrenaline junkie and like new challenges? Plan a new activity that pushes the boundaries every month. Maybe you find joy being with family and friends? Establish regular catch-up times so that you spend quality time with your nearest and dearest. Find the nectar wherever you can and make it an essential part of your every day.

Be more bee

Once you've identified what makes your heart sing, share the love. Like a bee showering pollen over the neighbouring flowers, you can do the same, by sharing your hopes and dreams with others and encouraging them to talk about the things they love. When we focus on the things we enjoy doing it lifts our spirits and helps to spread positive vibes.

Buzz

WORDS

—

Defy the odds; do it your way!

Feel the force

Let your wings beat out
a different kind of rhythm

Fly above the mire

Just bee you

'There is one masterpiece, the hexagonal cell, that touches perfection. No living creature, not even man, has achieved, in the centre of his sphere, what the bee has achieved in her own: and were someone from another world to descend and ask of the earth the most perfect creation of the logic of life, we should needs have to offer the humble comb of honey.'

MAURICE MAETERLINCK

More Than
A Woman

The Spice Girls may think they invented girl power, but the truth starts and ends with the bee. Making its first appearance almost 120 million years ago, the bee had female empowerment tied up quicker than you can say 'evolution'. With more than 25,000 species, organised into nine families, and in the case of honey bees a queen bee to rule the roost, there is no doubt that this divine mother is both the head and heart of the hive.

Revered and respected, her royal beeness has an entourage on wing to attend to all her needs. Usually much larger than the other bees, the voluptuous leader embraces her curves, for she knows this is the secret to her life-giving power. She is, after all, carrying a lifetime's worth of eggs. Family is everything, and her daughters are on hand to ensure she's fed and looking her best.

These worker bees – all female – are born ready. Gifted with all the skills they need to run the hive, they take multi-tasking to the next level, and while they may not do every available job, they'll progress through a series of different tasks during their busy lifetime. From cleaning cells and ventilating the hive, to attending to the queen and packing the pollen, these go-getting girls fly towards a challenge. Key decision-makers, they have the power to influence change in the form of a swarm, and when it comes to a new queen of the castle, they're the ones who decide on the time. They have the final 'buzz' word on everything, being first in line of winged defence, and in charge of security too. Thinking of crashing the hive for some honey? Think again. This is a private party, and if you're not coming in, you're not coming in, end of.

It's no wonder Ancient Greek goddesses caught the bee power bug and made it their own. With the bee as their emblem of choice, a symbol of power and majesty, these deities knew they were invincible.

In the temples of Artemis, Aphrodite and Demeter, priestesses were known as bees and called 'Melissae'. Wearing wings to worship, they praised the deity of their choosing as if she was queen bee and mother of all. This association grew over time, and soon honey bees in flight were considered messengers of the gods, a representation of the divine feminine force and all-round superwoman.

Be more bee

Express yourself. Don't be shy about how you feel. Share your thoughts and feelings, and if something doesn't sit well with you, say. It can be hard to stand up for what you believe is right, particularly if others don't agree, but make like the queen bee, who fights for her right to rule, and say how you feel and why. Even if nothing changes, you'll feel better for getting things off your chest and being true to your wonderful self.

Release the queen

You are the queen of your world, even if you don't always feel like it. Your home is your hive, and your family and friends are your co-worker bees. Harness your regal brilliance with this simple technique.

Stand in front of a full-length mirror. Look yourself in the eye and note your magnificence. Stand tall and imagine your spine gently lengthening. Notice how strong and determined you feel. Survey your reflection and pick out all your best features, for example your bright eyes, sense of style, gleaming skin. Acknowledge that you look good in your own skin and that your body works for you, every day, helping you achieve all your tasks. Imagine a sparkly crown balanced upon your head, which casts an aura of light over your entire image. Know that you are special. There is only one of you, and you are loved. Say 'I am queen bee!' with feeling. Repeat this affirmation until you really mean it.

Be more bee

Ensure you have a good support network of
female friends. Nurture those relationships
by spending time with them and enjoying their
company. If your schedule is busy, make a point
of touching base with a quick text or phone call
to find out how they are.

Take the lead

Be the head of the swarm and take the lead with these bee-inspired tips.

● See it and believe it. If you've a goal in mind, picture it as clearly as the sweetest, brightest flower swaying in the breeze. See yourself reaching it. Drink in the emotions and relive the narrative every day until that goal is in your grasp.

● Knowledge is power. Bees know what works and what keeps a colony thriving. Get to know everything about your area of interest. Read, watch, ask questions and learn from those who've travelled this flight path before.

● Be prepared for hard work. Every worker bee worth its pollen sac will tell you that nothing is gained by slacking. There are no short cuts to the sweetest pollen.

● Test your strengths. Worker bees have a go at anything. They learn on the job and put everything into each task; whether they're guarding the hive or cleaning up debris, their work ethic is the same, because every job is an important opportunity for growth.

'Let us turn elsewhere,
to the wasps and bees,
who unquestionably come
first in the laying up
of a heritage for their
offspring.'

JEAN-HENRI FABRE

Charge up your superpower

Fire on all cylinders, like a super worker bee, by activating the divine power within.

STEP ONE
Stand with your feet hip-width apart and your eyes closed.

STEP TWO
Roll your shoulders back and press your arms into your sides, as if you're holding a rolled newspaper under each armpit.

STEP THREE
Drop your weight down into your feet and bend your knees slightly.

STEP FOUR
Take a deep breath in and imagine you're drawing strength and energy from your core, up into the chest area. If it helps, bring your palms up level to your chest.

STEP FIVE
As you breathe out, turn your hands and push any negative energy down and away from your body.

STEP SIX
Continue this breathing technique for a few minutes, then when you feel relaxed, stand tall, give your body a shake and turn your attention to the space behind each shoulder blade.

STEP SEVEN
Imagine a pair of wings made up of tiny threads of light extending out from each shoulder. As each wing unfurls you feel a rush of energy surge through your body.

STEP EIGHT
Continue to breathe and enjoy feeling empowered and ready for anything.

Be more bee

Choose a goddess as your guru. Have fun exploring different mythologies and find a deity that you like or feel drawn to. Consider her qualities and how you can bring them into your own life. Is there a special plant, flower, stone or animal that she's associated with? If so, use this to tap into her energy. For example, Aphrodite's flower is the rose, so you might treat yourself to a bunch of roses once a month to lift your spirits.

Buzz

WORDS

—

Bee woman, bee fabulous, bee free

I am queen of me

Fly in the face of fear

Born fabulous, born ready!

My wings lift me up

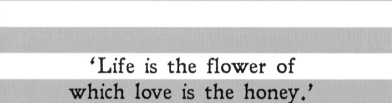

'Life is the flower of
which love is the honey.'

VICTOR HUGO

Hive Talking

If honey bees had a superpower, it would be their ability to engage. To give all their senses a workout. To eat, drink, dance and generally get their fill of the world. These sassy ladies know that you have to be on the money if you want the honey, so they make the most of what they've got, from bee-dy eyes, which help to locate the juiciest, most nectar-filled flower, to a keen sense of smell. Like a shopper hungry for a bargain at the first day of the sales, they can easily identify the good stuff – and whether it's been pillaged by a previous winged beauty. Second best is not an option for these girls. The motto is: be bold and go for gold.

On the ball, and on the bud, there is no dithering to be had; a forager bee knows exactly what she wants. This forthright lady appreciates the beauty of nature for what it is. The vibrant hue and shape of a flower head play a part in her selection process, along with the sweet odour and the fact that most nectar-laden blooms emit an ultraviolet light that this clever miss can detect. Once she's drawn to a specific bouquet, she'll alight and enjoy its natural loveliness, taking time to smell the roses, literally and metaphorically. Probing with her long tongue, known as a proboscis, she sucks the liquid and fills her belly. This can take several flower feasts, but this lady doesn't repress her appetite. No skinny measures here!

Nor is she a glutton, stealing all the best treats for herself. If the buffet table's groaning with a surplus of nectar, she'll tip off her BFFs back at the hive by getting jiggy with it, giving them a taste of what's in her bag, then throwing some shapes to reveal the location. Known as the 'waggle dance', this is a form of communication, so while she may not have moves like Jagger, her infamous twerk talks the talk and helps her sisters to walk the walk.

If her moves aren't up to scratch, which is highly unlikely as these girls take body language to the next level, there's always the pheromones. These chemical substances also help to get the message across, as well as ensuring she makes it home safely. Should the giddiness of excess make her lightheaded, a reassuring sniff of family steadies the flight and gets her tucked up for the night, because each bee colony smells distinctly different.

It's true that hunting for grub in nature's vast larder might not be high on our to-do list, but there's always something to strive for. Each day brings new challenges and treasures that we can enjoy. Blessings to be thankful for and moments to connect. With a little help from the bee, we can learn to dance with the flow of events and make the most of each toe-tapping, hip-waggling encounter!

Be more bee

Recreate a scene from memory, either in picture form, or as a poem or piece of prose. Relive the experience in your mind by once more engaging your senses and emotions and putting this into whichever creative form feels right for you. Using your senses and emotions in this way allows you to tap into the creative spirit and unleash your imagination.

Engage and excite

Take a moment and 'bee' at one with your surroundings with this simple technique.

STEP ONE
Find a spot outside, somewhere you can sit or stand comfortably and you won't be disturbed. Start by breathing deeply and make a note of how you feel in general at this point.

STEP TWO
Let your gaze fall on your surroundings. What do you see? Is there something that stands out? Perhaps an interestingly shaped tree, a pond, or a brightly coloured flower. Let this object become the focus of your attention for a moment.

STEP THREE
What do you notice about the object you've chosen? Take in its size, shape and texture. Consider how it might smell and how it might feel to touch. Imagine turning on your senses so that you can experience it fully.

STEP FOUR

Bring your focus to the rest of your surroundings.
Check in with your senses and notice what you
see, hear, smell, taste and touch.

STEP FIVE

Bring your attention back to you and your
breathing. Notice how you feel. Has there been
a change to your emotions?

Strike a pose

Who'd have thought the humble bee would be such an expert in non-verbal communication? A mistress of mime and mannerism, she knows how to connect with her team and get the best out of any situation, and you can do the same. Just catch on to the body language buzz and set your message in motion with these top tips.

● Be open and relaxed. Don't cross your arms or legs, as this acts as a defensive barrier. Instead, express yourself using open hands, and with your body facing the person you're talking to.

● Mirroring helps you form a connection with another person, so be sure to copy their movements and stance if you want them on side. This is something that happens naturally when we're in sync with someone and how they think.

● Encouraging movements like nodding and smiling help to promote success. Be sure to maintain eye contact as this shows you're interested in what the other person has to say.

● Try to keep your posture straight but relaxed. This shows that you are confident in yourself and what you have to say and will make the person you're talking to also feel relaxed and confident.

'Bees work for man,
and yet they never bruise
Their Master's flower,
but leave it having done,
As fair as ever and as fit to use;
So both the flower doth stay
and honey run.'

GEORGE HERBERT

Be more bee

Power up your thinking by matching gestures with words. Bees do this naturally using their body and their direction, pace and positioning during the waggle dance. When we do this we tend to express ourselves clearly, because hand gestures help us paint a picture and provide a direct link to speech. Practise in front of a mirror, particularly if you have a talk or presentation to deliver. It might feel strange at first, but once you get into the habit of doing this, you'll find it comes naturally and enhances your communication skills.

Activate bliss with a 'bee' list

To help you see and appreciate the beauty in your life, make a list of your blessings. Start small and simple, so things like the sun in the sky which lights your world, the ground supporting you, and the food and drink that sustain you, then move on to more personal elements like your friends, family, your unique gifts and talents, your career, the things you've achieved so far. Consider where you live, what you enjoy doing and the fact that you have the opportunity to do these things. Then move on to your daily routines, events that might have happened at work, like the colleague who gave you encouragement, the lovely lunch you had, or the delicious coffee that wakes you up every day. Add at least one new item to the list every day. Do this for a couple of weeks until it becomes second nature, enabling you to see and appreciate the blessings in your life.

Be more bee

Give yourself a nudge every now and then by
writing statements of gratitude on to sticky
notes and placing them where you can see them.
Some suggestions include a note saying 'I am
grateful for my natural beauty' stuck on the
bathroom mirror, or the phrase 'I am thankful
for a restful night's sleep' on your bedside table,
or 'I am grateful for the nourishing food I eat' on
the fridge door.

Buzz

WORDS

—

Bee bold, go for gold

Dance with the flow

Drink in each moment

Bee alive: see, feel, hear, touch, taste

Seek out beauty

'A swarm of bees in May is worth a load of hay, But a swarm in July is not worth a fly.'

BEEKEEPERS' PROVERB

You Should
Be Dancing

Pollination is contagious, just like dancing, and it's all thanks to the dynamic bee strutting its funky stuff. The ethos is simple: find something good and pass it on. Shimmying from flower to flower and plant to plant, these workers take part in a primal dance as old as time itself. They know how to mix it up. Each time they land, the pollen sticks to their super hairy bits and is passed on, pollinating flowers and plants (and thus the food we eat), and ensuring its future survival, contributing millions to the world economy in the process. Bees not only mean business, they make business, from the obvious pollination of crops, to the lesser, but equally charming, folk magic practised by our ancestors who believed bees to be a symbol of purity and wisdom.

The busy bumble is our friend in many ways, so much so that in ancient times it was considered good practice to tell the bees everything. Births, marriages and deaths – all significant events were relayed by the beekeeper to the hive so that they could spread the word. Babes born with the gentle touch of a bee upon their lips would become gifted speakers and poets, and for those fortunate to have one land upon their hand, a wealth of good fortune and abundance could be expected. A bee in the home meant the arrival of good news, or an unexpected visitor, but only if the bee was kept safe. Harming such a joyful treasure was more than frowned upon and could well incur the wrath of the gods, because bees are a blessing. End of.

These brightly striped superheroes keep the world going and growing, but just like Superman, they have their kryptonite. Modern insecticides, environmental factors such as the decline in foraging areas, and disease caused by the Varroa mite are just some of the issues sending them into deep decline. It's a lethal combination that's killing our honey bees in droves. It's up to you and all those in your hive to do something. Follow the flight path of the bee, work together, and make a world in which these mini marvels can thrive. Get buzzy and busy and pollinate the planet with positive energy and a renewed appreciation for the winged one. Dance and sing the praises of the bee that gives so much and asks for so little in return.

Positive pollination

Give it a go. Get the buzz trending by passing on positive energy to everyone you meet, physically and virtually throughout the day.

STEP ONE
Imagine a ball of golden energy in the centre of your chest. This represents your positive thoughts and feelings.

STEP TWO
Picture the ball of energy growing in size until it fills your chest with warmth.

STEP THREE

Whenever you interact with someone, whether face to face, over the phone or on email, draw light from this energy and bathe them in the glow. Do this by taking a deep breath in and, as you breathe out, imagine sending a stream of energy towards them.

This technique works both ways. The more positive energy you send out, the more you get back, so by the end of the day you'll be infused with joy!

Be more bee

Words are like pollen – they stick. Think carefully about your choice of words and what you say to yourself and others. Swap negative words for something more positive. For example, instead of berating yourself for not finishing a project by saying, 'I'm so stupid and slow,' replace this with a statement that looks at your strengths: 'I am thorough, creative and I care about my hobbies.'

Seven ways to save the bees

1 Say no to nasty insecticides.

2 Be garden compost savvy. Some composts contain a deadly insecticide called Imidacloprid, also referred to as vine weevil protection.

3 Go for bee-friendly plants: opt for wildflower seeds, and plant colourful, scented blooms and herbs to attract bees.

4 Create a safe haven in your garden by letting a small patch of land grow wild for the bees and other pollinators.

5 Invest in a bee box.

6 Support beekeepers by buying local honey.

7 Spread the word, sign petitions, get on social media and create a buzz!

'Every saint has a bee
in his halo.'

ELBERT HUBBARD

Be more bee

Become an advocate for the bee by making people aware of what they do for the planet. Just as the bee travels far and wide in its search for nectar and pollen, so you can spread the word and reach a wider audience by using every opportunity to educate, and make others aware of the bumble's plight. Think outside the bee box and have a bee-themed garden party. Invite friends and family, serve liberal amounts of honey with everything, and create your own 'save the bees' petition for them to sign.

Bee revived

Just like us, the busy bee gets tired and often needs a little help to get back to its buzzing best. If you come across an exhausted bee, give it a helping hand with this super simple elixir.

You'll need two tablespoons of white sugar and one tablespoon of water.

🔸 Mix the sugar and water together in a shallow saucer, then offer to the bee so it can take a sip.
🔸 Place it somewhere in the sun if possible, as the heat will also help to rejuvenate the bee.
🔸 Never offer honey as it may be imported and not suitable for your local garden bee.

And remember, just like the bee, look after your own needs on a daily basis. Regularly check in with how you feel and, if you find you're flagging, take a break and do something to lift your spirits, whether it's having a cuppa or a glass of water, getting out in nature, or spending five minutes chatting to your nearest and dearest. Deal with exhaustion before it takes over completely.

'When the flower
blooms, the bees
come uninvited.'

RAMAKRISHNA

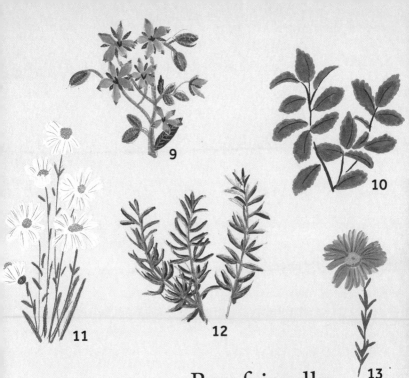

Bee-friendly flowers and plants

1 Cosmos	**8** Zinnia
2 Bluebell	**9** Borage
3 Thyme	**10** Mint
4 Primula	**11** Daisy
5 Lavender	**12** Rosemary
6 Sunflower	**13** Aster
7 Marigold	**14** Sage

Be more bee

To help bees stay hydrated, invest in some small ramekins. Add water or sugar solution to each, then place on top of your garden wall, or position them between patches of flowers, so that tired bees can take a sip whenever they need an energy boost! Alternatively, fill up a bucket with water and add some old corks to act as little floating landing pads for our thirsty, fuzzy friends.

Buzz
WORDS

—

Dance with joy
Pollinate positivity
Go bee-friendly
Get buzzy and busy!
Save the bees

'I always feel that I have missed some good fortune if I am away from home when my bees swarm. What a delightful summer sound it is! How they come pouring out of the hive, twenty or thirty thousand bees, each striving to get out first!'

JOHN BURROUGHS

I Started A Joke

Have you heard the one about the football-playing bumble bee? Sounds like a joke, but it's the truth. Wearing yellow and black, this player knows all the tricks to get the goal according to a research experiment carried out in 2017 at Queen Mary University, London. Bees like to play ball. They enjoy the challenge, and what's more these clever mites have learnt not only to copy each other but to develop their own strategies to score. During the experiment, bees watched a demonstration of how to get a ball in a hole, then followed suit, often paving the way by modifying their techniques and ball skills. Research also revealed these winged lovelies could count to four, use tools, and even learn foreign languages. It seems that while some behaviours are pre-programmed, such as the way they forage and communicate, others are learnt, making this ingenious creature the mastermind of the insect realm.

This is no surprise when you consider that they're also time lords, thanks to a nifty brain trick which reverses the ageing process. Yes, move over Dr Who, there's a new time traveller soaring through the skies in the form of the humble bumble. While age comes to all of us, the bee has learnt to embrace the process, going back to its youth by taking on jobs reserved for younger members of the hive. This in turn changes its brain chemistry and knocks off years. In other words, when you act young, you are young, making play a key factor in the quest for eternal youth!

With a brain the size of a seed, you might think the bee has little to offer in the way of intelligence. But size really doesn't matter. It's all about flexibility and giving the grey matter a workout. Whether they're interacting with the outside world, or navigating the darkness of the hive, our deep-thinking bees have learnt to adapt and go with the changes. Fleet of wing, foot and mind, they 'bend it like Beckham' on a daily basis and prove that even the super busy need to find time to explore, experiment and play if they want to defy the ageing process and boost brain power.

Be more bee

Clever bees copy and learn from each other. They take what they see and personalise it so that it works for them. Think about people you admire, those who always seem to be cheerful. What makes them tick? Perhaps they find the positive in every situation or have a laid-back attitude to life. Think of ways that you can emulate them and employ a similar approach. For example, take a step back and give yourself time out when you feel stressed, so that in time you'll worry less and relax more.

The joker of the hive

Jokes help us see the lighter side of life. Cultivating a sense of humour is like pollinating flowers and plants. You let the fun stuff rub off on you, and then pass on the laughter so that others can delight in the humour. It can be hard to see the funny side all the time, but these buzzing tips will get you in the right head space.

● Watch a comedy series or invest in a joke book, so that you get a dose of laughter every day.

● Have a go at making up your own jokes. Go through the alphabet and pick a different subject every day, then try creating a joke or witty pun about it. If you're struggling to think of something, try a play on words or a simple ditty. Anything that encourages you to be playful will help to change your frame of mind.

● Remember what it was like to be a child, how simple things made you laugh and smile. If something goes wrong, or doesn't work out how you'd planned, take a childlike approach and laugh it off. Tomorrow is a new day and every experience, good or bad, has something to teach us.

● Share the giggles. If you find something funny, let others in on the joke so that they can enjoy the fun and feel uplifted.

'The keeping of bees
is like the direction
of sunbeams.'

HENRY DAVID THOREAU

Play away!

Adopting a playful attitude can change the way you think and feel in a positive way. Go back to your childhood and experience a new zest for life. Start with a few simple questions.

● What did you love playing when you were a child?

● Were you a fan of being outside and active?

● Did you like board games?

● What kind of books did you enjoy reading?

● What kind of films did you enjoy watching?

● Did you enjoy spending time with groups of friends or solo?

● Were you a fan of dressing up and playing make believe?

● What did you want to be when you grew up?

Consider how you can bring some of that childhood joy into your life right now, perhaps by re-reading your favourite book, daydreaming about new adventures, or getting together with a large group of friends.

Be more bee

Job swapping is a regular occurrence in the hive. It's how bees stay young, active and move forwards. While you might not be in a position to swap jobs, you can alternate what you do with a colleague by switching some of their tasks with yours. The challenge will give you a boost, and you'll develop a new appreciation for the skills and talents of others.

Bee jokes

What does a bee call her sweetheart?
Honey

How do bees style their hair?
With a honeycomb

What did the angry bee say to her neighbour?
Buzz off!

What did the queen bee say to the naughty bee?
Bee hive!

What did the bee say to her boyfriend?
We bee-long together

What is the bee's favourite game to play?
Hive and seek

Which pop band do bees love the most?
The Bee Gees!

'It's wonderful to me that bees have this simple, age-old thing going on.'

PETER FONDA

Get your brain buzzing

Flexible bees know an active brain is a great asset when it comes to problem-solving, and it keeps them buzzing on all cylinders. Give your brain a workout by making random connections and exercising your memory at the same time.

STEP ONE
Write down one each of the following:

A fruit, a drink, a country, an animal, a song, a book, a mode of transport, a flower.

Pick the first thing that comes into your mind for each item.

STEP TWO
Give yourself five minutes to put all of the items you've chosen into a short story. Make it fun and be creative.

STEP THREE
Read the story several times out loud, so that you feel you know it.

STEP FOUR
Give yourself a break and go and do something else for a couple of hours.

STEP FIVE
Bring the story to mind and run through it, trying to remember all the random words you chose in Step One as you go. Write them down and see if they match your original list.

STEP SIX
Repeat, choosing different words, perhaps from books and magazines, and placing them in a short narrative. Practise every week and you'll have a magnificent memory worthy of the finest bumble, while also honing your creative skills.

Be more bee

Bees have the luxury of wings, which gives them height and perspective. We can gain the same thing by broadening our field of vision. Spend a few minutes every day looking out of the window. Take in what you see, then go further afield, beyond the view in front of you. Imagine you can go anywhere your mind takes you. Start by going up into the air and picture the view looking down. How different is it? Go higher, and then roam beyond your field of vision. Stretching your imagination and senses in this way can help you to be flexible in the way you think.

Buzz
WORDS

—

Bumble on!

Busy bees boost brain power

Play time delays time

Explore, experiment, experience!

Don't worry, bee happy!

'That which is not good
for the beehive cannot be
good for the bees.'

MARCUS AURELIUS

How Deep Is
Your Love

Bees are furry little pockets of joy. Round, fuzzy and a delight to the eye, the bee in all its glory is a sight to behold. What's more, they're big softies on the inside too. So while the sting has become a thing to be feared, the reality is much less sharp and more understated. Bees don't seek out trouble. Being armless and harmless, they rarely attack unless provoked. For to lash out means sudden death for the hardworking honey bee. It is only the queen that remains the most prolific warrior, whipping out her sting whenever she pleases, but even she is battle savvy, saving her best moves for those wishing to fight for her crown. The truth is, bees make peace and honey. It's what makes them tick.

Don't believe me? Gaze into the eyes of a bee and you'll gain a buzz buddy for life. Understandably, it's hard to know which eyes to look into first, for there are five, consisting of two compound and three simple eyes, which together detect light, dark and colour. Just like humans, bees are trichromatic, meaning they have three photoreceptors within the eye, but unlike humans, they can detect ultraviolet light. Cool enough, you might think, but there's even more to this optically talented bug than meets the eye(s). It has been discovered that the honey bee recognises human faces, taking parts like eyebrows, lips and ears and merging them together to make an entire visage. The process, known as configural processing, is so effective that it's being used to improve facial recognition software.

Let's face it, fellow humans, bees are ace at putting a name to the face, so while we may struggle to identify every different bee on the planet, they have no problem in getting to know their hive tribe.

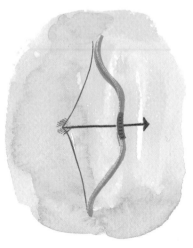

Gentle and graceful, these cuddly bumbles have found a way into our hearts. From the lilting buzz of their presence on a hot summer's day, to the way they pollinate and share their honey. Even bee venom has healing properties, for it contains molecules that increase levels of the anti-inflammatory hormone glucocorticoid. Everything about the bee is love. Everything they do, create and achieve is done to serve the hive and the greater good; proof enough that this intelligent insect really is the bee's knees of the animal kingdom.

Be more bee

Think of ways to assert yourself that are constructive and will help to ease tension. Balance your argument with positives and negatives, so you might applaud a partner or friend for something they've done well, while pointing out that they could have behaved in a different way which would have caused less stress. Try to see things from their point of view and remember that the person you're addressing is a member of your hive, whether they're a colleague, friend or close relative, so they should be treated with respect.

Rein in your sting

When bees sting it's a natural reflex and a defence mechanism because they feel under threat or need to stand their ground. Far from actively seeking to harm, bees use their sting as a last resort. Learn to do the same and retract rather than react.

STEP ONE
When tempers flare it can be hard to think rationally, so the minute you feel that first flash of anger, take a step back – physically and mentally. Imagine falling back inside your body.

STEP TWO
When we're agitated, we tend to take shorter breaths, which restricts the flow of oxygen to the brain and increases the heart rate. Turn your attention to your breathing and take slow, deep, breaths. This will also help you think clearly.

STEP THREE

The phrase 'seeing red' is often used to describe the onset of a tantrum. Red is the colour of action and aggression, while sky blue has a softer healing vibration, and pale pink is a loving shade. Depending on the situation and how you feel, imagine a wall of sky blue or pale pink descending in front of you. Picture yourself enveloped in this shade and notice how it makes you feel.

STEP FOUR

Insults may form in your mind when you're angry, and while you may feel they're necessary, things said in the heat of the moment are often a source of regret afterwards. Let the words come and go, like the ebb and flow of the tide. If it's possible, write down how you feel and pour all your anger on to the paper. Then leave it a few hours and re-read it. It's highly likely you won't feel the same measure of animosity.

Face up to it

What do you notice about someone when you first meet them? Do you really take in everything, or are you more bothered about the impression you're giving? Bees' powers of facial recognition are determined by the way they see, taking in separate details to make a fully formed picture. To make real loving connections with those in your inner circle, try these buzzing tips.

● When you meet someone for the first time, look at their face and take in as much detail as possible. As you do this, repeat their name in your head. This will help you to remember their name, should you meet them again.

● When spending time with those you love, be sure to take note of how they look. Non-verbal communication makes up 60–90 per cent of all communication, so check out visual signs and clues to ascertain how people are really feeling.

Smile – it's easier than a frown and more powerful than anything you could say.

Look into the eyes when you want to get a point across or really connect with someone. Humans have it easy, there being only two eyeballs to contend with. Bees have to work much harder with five!

Be more bee

Be interested and you'll 'bee' interesting! When you meet someone, whatever the scenario, remember to ask questions about them and their life. Show that you care by paying attention and being genuinely interested in what they have to say. Attentive bees always find the best flowers, a sentiment to consider when foraging for friendship and love.

Get your love buzz on

Bees never have off-days. The hive comes first in all things, which means a selfless take on life is guaranteed. What must be done is done from the heart with gusto, and all to a melody of gentle thrumming. It's no wonder love is in the air. Humans, being less crowd-orientated and more self-focused, can find it hard to feel and share the love, but there are ways of getting your love buzz on with a little insect-spiration!

Ask yourself:
- What can I do today to make someone else happy?
- What can I do today to show someone close I really care?
- How can I go about my daily business in a more loving and positive manner?
- What can I do to show I'm a team member?
- What could I change to feel more loving towards myself and others?
- Is there one thing I can do for someone else, just to be helpful?

'One can no more
approach people without
love than one can
approach bees without
care. Such is the quality
of bees . . .'

LEO TOLSTOY

Be more bee

Buzzing may be out of your vocal reach, but humming is similar in tone and feeling and creates the perfect musical backdrop for happy thoughts to thrive. Choose an upbeat tune and hum it under your breath as you get ready for the day. Feel the gentle vibrations in the back of your throat, and how the sound reverberates around your mouth. Experiment by switching tempo and volume and have fun with your humming. Come back to it at regular intervals during the day, when you have the opportunity, and notice how it makes you feel. If a negative thought pops into your head, try humming your tune and see how it changes your focus in a positive way.

WORDS

—

Believe in bees

Make peace and honey

Be the bee's knees

Less sting, more zing!

Get on the love buzz

'Handle a book as a bee does a flower, extract its sweetness but do not damage it.'

JOHN MUIR

Publishing Director Sarah Lavelle
Editor Harriet Webster
Designer Katherine Keeble
Illustrator Emily Mayor
Production Controller Sinead Hering
Head of Production Stephen Lang

Published in 2020 by Quadrille,
an imprint of Hardie Grant Publishing

Quadrille
52–54 Southwark Street
London SE1 1UN
quadrille.com

Cataloguing in Publication Data:
a catalogue record for this book
is available from the British Library.

text © Alison Davies 2020
illustrations © Emily Mayor 2020
design © Quadrille 2020

ISBN 978 1 78713 484 3

Printed in China

144